I0138035

A

# MONTH'S TOUR

IN

## NORTH WALES,
## DUBLIN,

AND ITS

## ENVIRONS,

WITH

## OBSERVATIONS

UPON THEIR

MANNERS AND POLICE in the Year 1780.

by

## Edward Lloyd

---

*Paucis ostendi oemis, et communia laudas;
non ita nutribus*

HOR.

---

London
Hounskull Publishing
2024

HOUNSKULL PUBLISHING
BM Box Hounskull
London WC1N 3XX

*A Month's Tour in North Wales, Dublin, and Its Environs*
Originally published in 1781.

First Hounskull edition published 2024
© Hounskull Publishing 2024

ISBN 978-1-910893-25-8

All rights reserved. No part of this publication may be reproduced, stored in a retrieval system, or transmitted, in any form, or by any means (electronic, mechanical, photocopying, recording, or otherwise) without the prior written permission of the publisher. Any person who does any unauthorised act in relation to this publication may be liable to criminal prosecution and civil claims for damages.

British Library Cataloguing-in-Publication Data:
A catalogue record for this book is available from the British Library.

This book is sold subject to the condition that it shall not, by way of trade or otherwise, be lent, hired out, or otherwise circulated without the publisher's prior consent in any form of binding or cover other than that in which it is published and without a similar condition including this condition being imposed on the subsequent purchaser.

# Table of Contents

# Note on This Edition

he text in this volume is based on the 1781 edition published in London by G. Kearsly. It is reproduced herein in its entirety.

The spelling and punctuation appear as in the original. Phrases in Latin that appeared in roman type have been rendered in italics; otherwise, the italics have been left untouched. Also unaltered is the capitalisation, except where that of place names was inconsistent; in these cases the capitalisation was harmonised. Minor spelling errors have been silently corrected. Missing words have been added, and footnoted accordingly.

A complement of editiorial footnotes has been added, and marked as such. A complete index has been generated.

# Preface

I t is observed by philosophers that human nature is nearly the same all over the globe; and it is proved by facts that there is much truth in the observation. The different degrees of cultivation, however, which we are blessed with, occasions as great a diversity in the face of the moral as of the natural world. Could we suppose these to be the same, we should probably find very little difference in mankind; one uniform appearance would be exhibited to the traveller's view, whatever regions he visited. But this is far from being the case. As nature is diversified with hills and vallies, fruitful fields and sandy deserts; so the complexion of the moral world varies exceedingly, according to the different, advantages of education, form of government, laws, customs, climate, &c. Here we see the mind overgrown with the wretched weeds of ignorance and barbarity, there we behold it adorned with all the virtues and graces of polished life mores.

While, therefore, the traveller's eye is employed in surveying the variety of scenes which nature exhibits, his attention thould be engaged in marking with accuracy the manners which characterize the inhabitants of those countries through which he passes; that, by selecting what ever is found excellent among them, he may learn to model his own conduct. Thus profit and delight will go hand in, hand, and, at the same time that he acquires health and chearfulness by a continual change of scene, he will daily and hourly lay up fresh treasures in his mind to meliorate and improve it.

Considered in this view, travelling must be of wonderful advantage. As there is no country which is all perfection, so there is no one which does not excel in some particulars, and from which a discerning person may not extract some good.

Nor do the advantages which invalids derive from travelling, deserve to be passed over in silence. To recommend it to them, it is sufficient to say, that it is an admirable specific against melancholy and ill-health, that the mind is fur-

nished; with a new train of ideas, the spirits re-
cruited, and the whole man becomes, as it were,
reanimated.

As it is presumed the following obervations
will never be exposed to the severe eye of crit-
icism, it is unnecessary to apologize for their
numerous imperfections, by mentioning the author's motive for writing them; which was merely
for the assistance of his own memory, and the entertainment of his worthy friend, at whose pleasing impulse he undertook the journey which gave
him an opportunity of making them.

> *Non recito cuiquam, nisi amicis, idque coac-*
> *tus.*[1]

Such were the author's origitial intentions.
But, prevailed on by the importunity of friends,
and thinking, as most authors do, that his work
would improve and entertain the public, he has
ventured to commit it to their candid perusal, es-
teeming it a peculiar happiness if he shall have in
the least contributed to these ends.

---

1    Horace, *Satires*, I, 4, 73: 'I recite to nobody but intimate
    friends, and then only when compelled.' —Ed.

# A Month's Tour, &c.

n the 19th of May I set out from an obscure village in Lancashire, in company with two very chearful and agreeable friends, and arrived at Chester to dinner. In the afternoon we took our route from hence to Holywell, passing through Hawarden and Northop, where we spent the night. The roads were extremely good, and the scenery beautiful. Nothing can excel the small county of Flint, either in pleasantness or fertility. The two fine rivers Dee and Mersey, the town of Liverpool, the ancient city of Chester, the insulated rock of Beeston, are objects which present themselves from almost every part of it.

In its bowels are mines of lead and calamine; on its surface, rich fields, woods and meadows.

On the 20th walked with Mr. W—— through a most delightful grove to the Copper-works, situate upon a fine crystal brook issuing from St. Winifred's Well, over which is a beautiful Gothic temple, supposed to have been built in the reign of King Henry the Seventh. Twenty-three mills are turned by this stream in he very small compass of about a quarter of a mile. Mr. Sm——by has lately erected here a fustian manufactory: the water is carried under his garden by means of a subterraneous arch. The spring is so copious, that eighty tons of water are emitted in the course of a minute.

After dining upon a quarter of lamb, and regaling ourserves with a bottle of generous port, we proceeded on our journey: but had not left Holywell before we met with an instance of British hospitality from the convivial Mr. St——ple. This honest Briton, a genuine descendant of Cadwallader, being an acquaintance of Mr. W——'s, waited for us at his gate, and insisted, with irresistible importunity, upon our drinking a glass of his ale.

After advancing about three miles from Holywell, we had a view of the seats of Messrs. Thomas and Pennant,[1] and Sir Roger Mostyn,[2]

---

1 Downing Hall, near Whitford, Flintshire. A fire damaged the house in 1922, following which it was never restored; it was demolished in 1953. —Ed.

2 Sir Roger Mostyn, 5th Baronet(1734 - 1796), a Whig politi-

all situate between the turnpike road and the sea shore.

The traveller's eye is here agreeably entertained with a most extensive and beautifully diversified prospect.

On the east are seen the rivers Dee and Mersey, the peninsula of Wirral, and the immense flat of Lancashire. On the north an extended tract of the sea, which we scarcely ever lost sight of, from Chester to the isle of Anglesea. On the west and south-west,

Hills peep o'er hills, and Alps on Alps arise.[3]

The next place we arrived at was Brekil, where was formerly held a respectable hunt. The rendezvous of the gentlemen was the Swan Inn, which is inclosed with a rail, lest the hogs, by a very natural blunder, should turn this residence of brave Nimrods into a filthy sty.

When we had proceeded a few miles further, the fertile and beautiful vale of Clwyd presented itself to our view. It runs nearly east and west, and from the mountains above Rythin to the sea at Ryddlan, is twenty miles in extent. No valley in Great Britain will admit of a comparisen with this. It is bounded by a lofty ridge of mountains

---

can, brother-in-law of Thomas Pennant (1726 - 1798). Plas Mostyn was demolished in 1963. At its former location there is now a cowshed. —Ed.

3    Alexander Pope, 'A Little Learning'. —Ed.

on the north and south, and is charmingly diversified with arable, pasturage, meadows, woods and water.

The river Clwyd flows through the midst of it. Denbigh is situate near the middle, and St. Asaph in the eastern part. At the latter place is a cathedral, but not remarkable either for its beauty or magnificence. They are, however, at this time expending a considerable sum in repairing and beautifying it.

Two miles from hence is Bottlewithin[4], the seat of Bennett Williams, esq. and about a mile from Kymmel, the residence of Mr. Roberts.[5] We proceeded from hence to Abergeley, without meeting with any thing worthy notice.

A small distance from hence, in the side of a hill, called Black and Blue, is a most extraordinary cave, concerning the extent of which the following curious anecdote is related. In order to discover the length of it, four men, it is said, carried with them three pounds of candles, which were consumed before they had reached the further end of it. Two only of the adventurers returned. Nor is it known to this day what became of the rest of them.

As we advanced, the beautiful castle, town, and vale of Conway, gradually displayed themselves to our view. Our carriage did not pass the

---

4    Bodelwyddan. —Ed.

5    David Roberts had recently purchased the Kinmel estate from Sir George Wynn for £42,000. —Ed.

river. At high water the ferry plies opposite to the town. As the tide was out at this hour, we were under the necessity of descending about a quarter of a mile, from whence we were ferryed to the town for a shilling each passenger.

The river of Conway is remarkable for fine salmon, and is navigable to Llanrwst. On the east side the water, nearly opposite to the town, are the following seats: Marle,[6] the property of Lawyer Walsh; Tregannion, adjacent to the sea, the refidence of Mr. Stoddard, Postgallon, belonging to Sir Roger Mostyn; and Glodydd, the seat of Mrs. Mostyn; all of which are pleasantly situated in view of Conway, the sea, and both the Ormsheads, &c.

We arrived at Conway about eight o'clock in the evening, and took up our residence at Mr. Read's, the Bull's-Head Inn. Mrs. Read is a native of Cheshire, extremely loquacious, and rather extravagant in her charge. She waited upon us with great condescension at supper, and in a most superfluous and distressing manner.

On the 21st got up at six in ths morhing to take a survey of the town. Conway is situate on the west side of the river, is a corporation town,

---

6    Marle Hall is said to have originally been built in 1661, the then and present version of it dates from the early 18th century, when it was expanded in the Georgian style. At the time of Lloyd's visit, and until the end of the 19th century, it was roofless and derelict on account of a fire in the middle of the 18th century, except for the east wing, which had remained inhabited. —Ed.

governed by a mayor, alderman; and bailiff of the castle. It is surrounded by a very strong wall, said to have been formerly adorned with fifty beautiful towers, several of which are still remaining. On the south-east is built a fine tower, whose foundation is solid rock, not greatly impaired outwardly, except the south side; where a large heap is fallen from the lower part of the wall, on account of its being undermined by the inhabitants, who blasted the foundation rock, in order to get stone for building.

The castle was s built by King Edward the First. Oliver Cromwell erected a battery, on an advantageous eminence, at about the distance of a quarter of a mile south of the town. His attempts to take it proved ineffectual for several years. The balls he made use of appear to have been nine pounders, several of which are preserved at Conway, being found by digging in gardens. These made but a very light impression on the castle. But what Oliver was not able to effect by force, he accomplished by cunning.

He destroyed the leaden pipes, by means of which water was conveyed to supply the town, and so starved them into compliance.

We breakfasted at eight, and left Conway. The ascent of Penmaen-Ross from the town is gradual, the descent on the other side steep; but the terror is greatly extenuated by a good stone wall, which is carried from hence till we passed Penmaen-maûr. This is a most tremendous mountain, shooting up almost perpendieularly into the skies. He topples in some parts over his base, and threatens the traveller with impending ruin. He is beset with rugged cliffs, and cover'd with rude stones of a prodigious size. Opposite to Penmaen is an arch to support the road, of most excellent workmanship, and durable materials.

After passing a small village called Llanber,[7] the linch-lin of the hind wheel of our carriage was lost, and we met with numberless interruptions from it, till we arrived at Bangor. We were under the necessity of walking near a mile. Our misfortunes, however, were greatly alleviated by the consoling reflection that we had passed the steep precipice before this accident happened to us, otherwise we must, in all human probability, have perished.

We arrived at Bangor about eleven, and breakfasted a second time after which we attended divine service at the cathedral. This edifice is very plain, but neat. Here is a very musical organ, the workmanship of Mr. Green, which cost three hundred and sixty guineas.[8]

---

7    Llanfairfechan? —Ed.

8    This organ had been built the year before, in 1779, when the 1660 organ was replaced. That earlier organ was itself a replacement of the original from between 1350 to 1370, which had been removed or destroyed during the Commonwealth by Parliamentary order "for the speedy demolition of all organs, images and all matters of superstitious monuments in all cathedrals . . . throughout the kingdom of England and the dominion of Wales." Samuel Green's or-

After morning service we proceeded in our Conway chaise to the ferry, crossed over into Anglesey, took a fresh carriage at Carter's, and having advanced a mile, enjoy'd a distinct view of Sir N. Bailey's seat, which is pleasantly situate about two miles south-west of the Holy-head road.

The island continued rather pleasant, and tolerably fertile, save in the article of timber, till we reached Gwindu. Here we met with a truly hospitable reception from Mrs. H——s, who has united the obliging air of the Inn-keeper with the ease and good breeding of English ladies. Here is the largest cat we ever beheld she measures from the head to the extremity of the tail a yard and an inch, and is sixteen inches high. Her colour is grey.

We left Gwinda at six, and arrived at Holyhead little before eight. This part of Anglesey exhibits a very dreary appearance. It is a plain country, but abounds with rocks, which seldom shoot much above the surface of the earth, and is, for the most part, covered with furze near the road side. Within three miles of the Head we crossed a navigable channel, which divides the island into two unequal parts.

Holy-head is a small town in the most western part of Anglesey, has a church, and a market on Saturdays. Here are stationed five King's packets,

der was replaced by William Hill's, which was installed in 1873, added to in 1897, rebuilt in 1954, and remains in use till present day. —Ed.

(sloops of seventy or eighty tons burden) which sail every day, except Thursdays, for Dublin.

On the 22d we embarked on board the *Dartmouth*, Captain Hartwell, at two o'clock A.M. When we weighed anchor, the wind was south-west, very favorable for Dublin, which is situate exactly north-west of this port.

We and the rest of the passengers, which consisted of three land officers, a sergeant, and a servant, four Jesuits, a lady, and a young boy, were in high spirits, expecting to arrive at Dublin in eight hours. But experience soon taught us that there is no depending upon the uncertain elements to which we had now committed ourselves.

There was a prodigious swell in the sea and when we had advanced six leagues, the wind changed to the west, and continued near this point for some time, inclining, however, to the north. At noon it changed to the north-west, and blew with great violence for the space of twenty hours. The billows rolled mountains high, and it was with the utmost difficulty that the ship made head against the turbulence of the storm.

At three o'clock, P. M. we made the Hibernian shore.

We steered to the north, in order to get the tide upon our lee bow, which render'd our passage the more dangerous, as well as tedious, being obliged to make several tacks to gain the wind. In the mean time we were assailed by several squalls of wind, attended by a perpetual succession of hailstorms and rain, the wind till continuing north-west. At nine P. M. we stood with our bow south-south-west, the wind still blowing with increasing violence. We kept this course for several hours. At four A. M. we were under the necessity of heaving the ship to, in order to take in an additional reef in our main and foresail. When we had done this, we endeavoured, by plying to windward, to make the Dublin bay, and at half past five A. M. open'd it, and came to anchor at eight off Dunleary, two leagues from Dublin.

Notwithstanding this toilsome and dangerous passage, the mariners, who were all Welshmen, except the Captain, were never observed to swear au oath, which reflects no small honour upon him and his men.

All the passengers were sea-sick, save Mr. W——, who continued upon deck till nine P. M. All the rest consigned themselves to their beds very early, and a profound silence, save where silence yielded to the eructations of qualmish stomachs, reigned in the cabin till six o'clock on Tuesday morning.

On the twenty-third, when the pleasing news was brought to the sickly inhabitants of the cabin, that the ship was making way very fast, the officers and Jesuits began ro regale their empty stomachs with cold tongue, fowl, wine, grog, &c. particularly the latter, who gorged themselves most enormously close to my bed-side, deafen-

ing me at the same time with an elaborate disser-
tation upon snuff.

There was something peculiarly disgusting in
the appearance of these people their countenanc-
es scemed to discover very black designs. But as
this is not an infallible criterion to judge by, I was
inclined to think more favourable of them. We
got into a small boat at half past ten, and landed
at George's quay at two P. M.

The port of Dublin has received no advantages
from nature, but nothing that art could do has
been withheld from it. A beautiful stone wall, and
wooden piles, extend three miles into the bay, on
purpose to confine the water, and make it of a
proper depth for ships to pass the bar. After all,
it is still a very incommodious harbour to enter.
From the bay, however, a finely diversified scene
is presented to the eye. The hill of Howth, the
city of Dublin, the town of Black Rock, Clintorf
and Dunleary, a number of white edilices erected along the shore and upon the mountains, well
cultivated fields, and rising grounds, form one of
the most delightful prospects in Europe.

As soon as we disembarked, we were happy to
dine at the Marine coffee house. After dinner we
took coach, and proceeded to our lodgings at Mr.
V——'s in Parliament fireet, where our worthy
friend Mr. B—— met us, and accompanied us
to the Exchange. This is a very magnificent and
elegant building planned by Mr. Cooley.[9] The

---

9    At the time Thomas Cooley (1740 - 1784)'s exchange build-

four orders of architecture are here displayed in a very masterly manner, and the whole structure does him great honour.

Opposite the entrance of the north front, on a white marble pedestal, is a statue in brass of his present Majesty, executed by Mr. Van Nost. As we ascended the geometrical stair-case of the Exchange, an excellent statue,[10] in honour of the patriotic Dr. Lucas, holding Magna Charta in his hand, presented itself to our view. This edifice cost 70,000*l.* five thousand of which was allowed by governmen.

After coffee, which greatly alleviated chat painful dizziness the motion of the ship had left in our heads, we walk'd to Stephen's Green, a beautiful gravel walk shaded with trees, including a large field, in the centre of which is an equestrian statue of King George the Second.[11] The houses are in general well built, but not uniform. The circumference of the square is a mile.

On the twenty-fourth we breakfasted at the Old Exchange coffee-house, and visited our agreeable acquaintance Mr. Mrs. and Miss P——. From hence we went to Patrick's cathe-

---

ing was recently completed: it was built between 1769 and 1779. —Ed.

10   By Edward Smyth, 1772. —Ed.

11   Completed by John Nost the Younger in 1756 and erected in 1758, the statue was vandalised around 1814 - 1815, and bombed by the IRA on Remembrance Sunday 1928 (with minimal damage) and again on 13 May 1937 (this time blowing it to pieces), following which it was removed. —Ed.

dral, an ancient venerable edifice, erected in honour of and dedicated to St. Patrick, in the year 410, after he had preached the gospel at Dublin.

On the south side of the aisle are the busts of the celebrated Dean Swift, and Mrs. Johnson, or Stella. On the north side is the monument of Dr. Smith,[12] with beautiful pillars of Egyptian marble, fluted in the Corinthian order.

On the south side the altar is a Gothic monument, of a most enormous size, in honour of Sir Richard Boyle, Lord Orrery, Earl of Cork, his Lady and children. The height of it is about twelve yards. He died in 1629.

From the top of St. Patrick's steeple, we had a delightful view of the city and the adjacent country.

Near this is the public library, an elegant room, containing a tolerable collection of books.

From hence we proceeded to the exhibition of pictures, where we saw but few pieces of extraordinary merit.

We next visited Trinity college. It is four stories high, and has twenty-three windows in front. The first quadrangle is of Portland stone, similar to the grand one at Christ church in Oxford. The second is not remarkable either for beauty, size or elegance. The third is a very spacious; one, built partly of brick and partly of stone. The

---

12    Arthur Smyth (1706 - 1771), Archbishop of Dublin between 1766 and 1771. The monument is in the south transept of the cathedral. —Ed.

hall is large, but has no pretensions to elegance. The chapel is very plain. The library is a fine lofty room, adorn'd with pillars of Irish oak, and furnished with a good collection of books.

The college consists of a Provost, six senior and eighteen junior Fellows, and sixty scholars. The Provost's lodgings are very stately and commodious.

The part of Trinity, however, which most engaged our attention, was the anatomical school, in which is a set of figures in wax, representing, in a manner peculiarly striking, females in every state of pregnancy. They are done upon real skeletons, and are the labours of almost the whole life of a most ingenious French artist named Denoue. This monument of uncommon genius cannot fail to transmit his name to posterity with the brightest lustre.

They were purchased by the late Lord Shelburne,[13] and presented to the college.

The museum contains objects of real curiosity, besides an Egyptian mummy, which is very well preserved. This edifice was erected in 1591.

Opposite to the college are both houses of Parliament, which without exhibit rather a heavy appearance, as there are several large pillars, which have apparentl little to support besides a very low dome.[14]

---

13 John Petty Fitzmaurice, 1st Earl of Shelburne (1706 - 1761). —Ed.

14 Designed by Edward Lovett Pearce (1699 - 1733), and built

The house of Commons consists of three hundred members; it is extremely neat and commodious, of an octagon form, and has a pleasant gallery, from whence spectators may hear the debates with much comfort.

The house of Lords consists of an hundred and sixty-two members and is more remarkable for its convenience, than beauty and elegance.

The blue-coat school, an academy for the instruction of citizens sons, is a very handsome edifice; but at present in an unfinished state.

The house of Industry is large, and well regulated.

The new prison is built upon an excellent plan, each criminal having a seperate cell, and being, therefore, in no danger of becoming, by evil communication, more than when they entered.[15]

In the course of this morning's ramble, we saw several beautiful streets, particularly Dominiq-

---

in 1729, this was the world's first purpose-build bicameral parliamentary building (the House of Parliament in London was a converted building and the House of Commons was previously a chapel, hence MPs facing each other). It ceased to function as houses of parliament following the Act of Union 1800, when Ireland became part of the United Kingdom of Great Britain and Ireland. Since 1803 it has housed the Bank of Ireland. —Ed.

15  Built between 1773 and 1781 on the design of Thomas Cooley, Newgate Prison, as this was called, was intended to replace a former iteration of the same name, previously located in a converted city gate marking Dublin's western boundary, 180 ft / 55 m south of Brown's Castle gate (which itself served as Black Dog prison). Newgate was closed in 1863 and the building used as a vegetable market until its demolition in 1893. —Ed.

15

ue's and Sackville's: the latter is very spacious, well-built, and in the midst of it is a mall, inclosed by a low wall. At the west end of this street, but (which is greatly to be lamented) not in a line with it, is situate the Lying-in hospital. This was erected and endow'd at the expence of Mr. Moss, surgeon and man-midwife, who began this humane edifice at a time when his finances did not exceed seven hundred pounds, and persisted, in spight of poverty itself, till he had completed it.

Near this is the rotunda,[16] built by the charity of the same liberal. gentleman. This is an imitation of the London Ranelagh upon a small scale. We were at night agreeably entertained here with singing by Mess. Johnson and Conor, together with concertos by Mess. Pinto, Padra, &c. The company was numerous. and brilliant.

The profits arising from this place of elegant entertainment, are appropriated to the support of the above-mentioned, hospital.

We next visited the barracks.[17] This is a noble and useful structure, consisting. or one quadrangle and three courts, having each three wings, and calculated for the accommodation of six thousand soldiers. We were fortunate enough to reach this at the time the officers were drawing up their men to attend the Lord Lieutenant to the house.

---

16    Designed by James Ensor and completed in 1767. —Ed.

17    Collins Barracks, which now houses the National Museum of Ireland—Decorative Arts and History. —Ed.

His present Excellency would be a very unpopular character in Ireland, was it not for his Lady's connections, who is sister to Mr. Conolly, a gentleman of considerable rank, fortune and popularity. His Lordship discovers, upon all occasions, a contracted spirit in his œconomical expences, which, of all passions, notwithstanding he may have private reasons for it, is the least fitted for the support of regal dignity. He is, however, no enemy to pomp. The procession was conducted with a magnificenee not at all inferior to that with which the King is attended when he goes to the house of Lords.

We spent so time and pains this day in gratifying our curiolity, that our strength and spirits were nearly exhausted with hunger and fatigue. Against these an excellent remedy was provided by our very worthy, friend Mr. B—— the younger, whose good sense, sprightliness, and hospitality, are scarcely to be paralleled. He treated, us with a good dinner, claret, whisky, (which js prepared from the juice of malt put into the still without being hopped) and persico, a very pleasant liquor, made ol the juice of lemons, oranges, brandy, and various other ingredients, refined by milk.

We supped at D——s tavern, where we were very well accommodated with eatables, porter, and black strap, or punch made of currant whisky.

On the twenty-fifth we engaged a chariot, and set out, in company with Messrs. T—— and

B———, for Lipzlip, a small town situate seven Irish (nine English) miles[18] west of Dublin. In our road we had a view of the, Bishop of Derry's seat, the King's lodge, Phœnix park, and a few neat villas belonging to Dublin merchants.

We pass'd by Strawberry gardens, which beginning at Chapelizod, extended four miles along a fine sunny bank near the road side. The inhabitants of Dublin are supplied from hence with plenty of this wholesome and delicious food.

About the five mile stone, in a small grove, is a spa of similar properties to the Harrowgate water, but not so strongly impregnated.

When we arrived at Lipzlip, our appetites were wonderfully keen, and we ate eggs, and drank tea, with perseverance.

Near this town is situate Lord Massereene's seat,[19] upon a most romantic eminence, near the

---

18    The Irish mile, used in plantations from 16th century until the 19th century (with some residual use in the 20th), was based on the English measure, but, instead of using a rod of 5.5 yards, it used a linear perch of 7 yards, which resulted in a mile that was 1.27 statute miles, or 2,240 yards / 2.048 kilometres long. —Ed.

19    Antrim Castle. First built in 1613, it was at the time of Lloyd's visit, still in its Restoration guise, following John Clotworthy (the 1st Viscount Massereene)'s enlargement of 1662. In 1813 it was rebuilt and in 1922 it was destroyed by a fire, which was suspected to have resulted from an IRA arson attack, but following which, evidence of arson being inconclusive and insurance therefore not paid out, remained in ruins until demolished in 1970. The hexagonal tower built during the enlargement of 1887 still stands. —Ed.

barks of the Liffey. Here is a delightful walk in a grove close to the water side, shaded by trees, which conducted us to a beautiful fall of water called the Salmon-leap, far inferior to that at Bally-Shannon, which is fourteen yards perpendicular height. This is formed by the Liffey rushing through an arch; and tumbling down a rock of a considerable height.

The rudeness of nature is: here so jutliciously chastised by art, that the place exhibits a scene highly pleasing and picturesque. I was delighted with it to such degree, that with regret

> ——These deep solitudes, and awful cells,
> Where heav'nly-pensive Contemplation dwells.

In the house we saw several good paintings, and from che top of it were presented with a great variety of agreeable prospects. It is at this time inhabited by the Lady Dowager Massereene, whose son has been confined in France since about the conclusion of the last war, for having attempted to set some of the French docks on fire.[20]

In our return from hence our patience was fairly put to the trial.

It has been observed that the Irish peasantry are an indolent, lazy tribe; and, if it were right to form our judgment of a whole people from a

---

20  He would be freed by a mob on 13 July 1789, a day prior to the storming of the Bastille. —Ed.

single individual, the instance we now met with would abundanily prove the fact.

We set out from Dublin at eight o'clock in the morning, and it was almost noon when we arrived at Lipzlip. Nor were we at all more expeditious in returning. Our charioteer was such a composition of impudence and laziness as it is to be seldom met with. When we requested him to accelerate his pace, he took no notice of what we said to him. When he came to the most trifling ascent, he descended from the box, opened the carriage door, and offered to hand us out without any further ceremony.

The cause of their tardiness may be in a great measure attributed to the manner of paying them by the hour, sixteen pence the first, and eight pence after, during the whole journey. If it was their interest to travel fast, they would in time shake off their native slothfulness; as it is, are likely to improve in it.

In the course of his excursion, we had an opportunity. of proving the truth of another observation not much to the credit of the Irish, that they are great swearers.

Our landlord at Lipzlip was a singular instance of this: his ordinary language consisted of little else but oaths. They do not, like other countries, confine the use of them to express indignation, but intermix their common discourse with them, even in their coolest moments, and utter the most horrid imprecations when they assert a thing with any degree of vehemence.

This, however, is chiefly applicable to the inferior ranks.

After dining at D——s, we walked for recreation to the bason, which is situate at the west end of the city, near the navigation intended to communicate with the Shannon.

A porter constantly attends this walk, who admits none but such as make a genteel appearance.

Here we spent an hour very agreeably in contemplating the beauty of the propect, and the far more enchanting beauty of certain moving objects that pass'd in review before us while we sat down. Our very worthy and good-natured friend Mr. B—— junior introduced us to Miss B——, the celebrated Dublin beauty, whom few behold with impunity. The admirable proportion of her form, and delicacy of her complexion, can scarcely be surpass'd even in the finest imagination.

On the 26th we visited the royal hospital, a very munificent establishment for the relief of superanuated soldiers, or such are otherwise disabled in the service of their King and country. It was erected by Charles the Second, and the first stone of it laid by the Duke of Ormond, who was then Lord Lieutenant. Here is a fine spacious hall, adorned with several valuable paintings, particularly a figure of Sir Cecil Wicke, executed by Rubens. On che all are 1 four hundred stands of arms, which is the number of pensioners the establishment admits of.

The chapel is very magnificent. The Gothic altar in it is truly venerable. The wood is ingeniously carved, and the stucco of the roof most curiously wrought.

We were presented from the top of the Hospital with an excellent view of Dublin, Phoenix park, the King's lodge, Knock castle, and the rising mountains in the county of Wicklow, covered with verdure to the top.

The long walk is shaded with two rows of venerable lime trees.

Contiguous to this, seperated only by a wall, is a burying ground, which, in ancient times, belonged to the Knights Templers of Jerusalem, and wherein was lately found a monument of one of the Kings of Munster. It is a stone about twelve feet long, and two in breadth.

At the west of this burying ground is a tower, with a large cistern, containing an hundred hogsheads of water, for the supply of the hospital.

The plan of this edifice was taken from the Hospital of Invalids at Paris. The revenue arises from the deductions made out of the pay of military officers.

The next place we visited, was the Foundling Hospital, a most entensive charity for the reception of orphans of every denomination, from any part of the globe.

They need no other recommendation to be admitted here, but to bear the form of the human species. There is a nurse appointed to receive them, who is not authorised to make any enquiries whatever. No less than an hundred and fifteen infants were received, about two months ago, in the course of eighteen days. They are put out to nurse till they are three or four years of age, the number of which at this time is three thousand.

They are generally brought here with labels round their necks, on which their names are inscribed.

The nurses are frequently so attached to these forlorn babes, that they adopt them for their own children; when this does not happen, they are returned to the hospital, where they are instructed in all the useful arts of life, till they become of a proper age to be sent out as apprentices.

The money arising from licensing carriages, &c. is applied to the support of this humane institution.

Not far from hence is the Lunatic Hospital,[21] to the founding of which the celebrated Dean Swift left eleven thousand pounds.

We dined at D——s, where the facetious Mr. St——ns entertained us greatly with his Caledonian jokes, scarlet coat, and moral contenance.

After drinking tea at the Exchange coffee house, and spending the remainder of the evening an our own apartments, we retired to

---

21   St. Patrick's Hospital for Imbeciles, founded in 1757, and modelled after St Mary of Bethlehem in England, was the first institution for the mentally ill in Ireland. —Ed.

our beds very early; but our sleep was so inter-
rupted by the hoarse voice of riot and discord,
from which the streets of Dublin are scarcely ever
free, that we enjoyed but little repose this night.
Mr. T—— got up to his window, and address d
the rioters in menacing terms, but to very little
purpose; at which time he was an eye-witness
to such a scene of indecency as would shock any
chaste ear to relate.

The greatest part of the morning we amused
ourselves with reading, writing, &c. and din'd
at D——s. The meat was extremely ill-cooked,
which so much disconcerted Mr. T——, that he
recovered not his accustomed good-humour the
whole evening. The waiter brought him young
cabbages run up into about a foot in length, as
green sauce to his veal and bacon.

Mr. B—— did us the pleasure of spending
the evening at our lodgings, and favour'd us with
many a pleasant ditty.

On the 28th it was our intention to attend divine service at St. Patrick's but were prevented
by the vexatious dilatoriness of our barber. After
this disappointment, we composed ourselves as
well as we could, and accompanied Mr. P——to
Christ Church.

The service was perform's in the usual solem-
nity of cathedrals and a sermon by Dean Coote.

On the south side of the[22] aisle are the following monuments; viz.

---

22   'of the' missing in the original. —Ed.

1. That in memory of the late Lord Chancellor Bowes, a statue of Justice sitting, in white marble.

2. That in honour of Thomas Prior, a very worthy private gentleman, Van Nost sculpsit 1756. It represents his bust between two boys, in white marble, one of which is weeping, and the other holds a scroll.

3. A little below this lies, extended in full proportion, Richard Lord Strongbow, the first and principal invader of Ireland, Lord of Chepstow, &c. He died at Dublin in the year one thousand one hundred and seventy seven: the part of a person. which lies beside him according to the uncertain reports of tradition, represents his son, whom he is said to have cut through for want of courage: or, according to some, it represents his wife Eva. The antique appearance of these figures is totally ruined by white paint.

On the north side the altar is erected a very stately monument in memory of the Earl of Kildare, the present Duke of Leinster's grandfather.

The Earl lies extended. At his head are represented, in full proportion, his relict and daughter standing over him in a most pensive attitude. At is feet is the late Earl wringing his hands in a very affecting manner. This was executed by Cheere.

After service we walk'd to Stephen's Green, which was crouded wich much genteel company.

We dined at Mr. P——s, went to St. Anne's to evening service, and returned to our worthy friend Mr. P——s to tea. The remaining part of his sacred day was spent at our lodgings, where we supped upon the largest and best cockles we had ever tasted.

On the 29th we were greatly disappointed in finding no marks of public joy and festivity upon this day, except the firing of the guns in Phoenix park. There was not a branch of oak to be seen, and scarcely a set of bells heard to ring throughout the whole city.

We dined and drank tea at Mr. W——s, Quaker, in whom we met with a very sensible and agreeable host, but quite debilitated by the gout. In lamenting the inactive life he lead, he observed, that neither animals nor vegetables could possibly subsist long without exercise. Labour, natural or artificial, is absolutely necessary to the animal economy,—winds and gentle breezes to the support of vegetable life.

In the former, labour promotes a proper circulation of the blood and fluids;—in the latter, winds and breezes, which serve as their exercise, cause a just distribution of the juices into every part of plants.

Any one that visits Dublin, must observe, that Quakers are not that precise, unsocial set of mortals here, which they are in some parts of England. They sing a chearful song, frequent assemblies and other polite places of entertainment promiscuously with the rest of their fellow citizens. One of the youthful tribe being reprov'd by a primitive elder for his love of music, reply'd, "that it is the characteristic of taste and genius to be an admirer of it; for among all che beasts of the field, none are insensible to the charms of music—except the Ass."

However, notwithstanding the general sociableness of their dispositions, the Quakers, in order to preserve that strict union, which this sect above all others maintain among themselves, take particular care to instil into the minds of their offspring a tender concern for their own community, and a total disregard for all others. A convincing proof of this appeared at Mr. W——s table. A child of seven years old, ignorant of the art of disguising his sentiments, told a person of the church of England, who sat by him, "he wish'd all the wine, bottles, and glasses, on the table, were in his belly." Upon his telling him they would soon put an end to his life—his answer was "he did not care for that because (says he) thou art no friend of ours".

We spent the evening with our sprightly, open-hearted friend Mr. B——, where we were regaled with a luxurious supper, excellent claret, whisky, persico, &c. The Reverend Mr. P——, a lively and agreeable companion, entertain'd us with a multiplicity of songs of his own composing, and which bore evident marks of the native vivacity of his temper. The evening was concluded with a glass to the glorious memory of King William. The respect they bear the name of that monarch falls but little short of adoration. There is a fine equestrian statue of him in College Green, whose sides are adorned with warlike trophies.

On the 30th we amused away the morning in reading, writing, &c. Dined and drank tea at Mr. P——; and, after spending several hours here in chearful and agreeable chat, we concluded the evening in the character of spectators at the Lord Lieutenant's ball. The room is elegant, and hung with a rich, tho' not gaudy paper. It is furnished with five glass *chandeliers*. The benches, which extend the whole length of the room, are covered with green moreen, except the front ones, which are occupied by the female nobility, the covering of which is scarlet.

At the upper end of the room the Lord Lieutenant and his Lady sit enthron'd, with their pages and *aids de camp* standing behind them.

The company was not very numerous but the ladies, as is universally the case at Dublin, were well dressed, and danced with much vivacity.

I cannot help a that there is more smartness than truth in Mr. Twiss's observation upon the ladies' legs.[23] He should have confined his censure to females of inferior rank, the thickness whose legs may be attributed partly to their

---

23  In *A Tour in Ireland in 1775*, Richard Twiss writes: 'As to the natural history of the Irish species, they are only remarkable for the thickness of their legs, especially those of the plebeian females.' —Ed.

wearing neither shoes nor stockings in their infancy, and partly to the far greater exercise they
undergo than those whom fortune has exempt-
ed from labour. As to the higher ranks, the English have very little superiority to boast of in this
particular. Nor do they fall greatly short of them
in any female accomplishment, unless we class
fortune under this denomination. The Irish ladies, like the other sex, are free and open-hearted; and, at the same time that they discounte-
nance ill-bred familiarity, are very far reen from
reservedness.

On the 31st we sat out in a coach and four early this morning, for the county of Wicklow. About
the fifth mile-stone is a very great curiosity called
the Scalp, where the road penetrates through the
midst of a mountain of the same craggy complexion as Paemaen-mawr. Under the rigged
rocks are heard the murmurs of a subterraneous
brook, which emerges at a small distance near
the road side.

Aster passing the ninth mile-stone, we got out
of our carriage, and walked to the Dargle, thro' a
field deliciously-scented with furze blossoms.

As we descended the Dargle, or Dingle, we entered a wood where a fine natural scene, truly romantic and picturesque, discovered itself.

The sides of the Dargle are beautifully covered
with woods. At the bottom flows a brook which
murmurs at the interruptions it meets with from
stones and rocks. About the middle is the lover's

leap, a large rock which shoots up in the form of a castle to a great height.

Near this, at the side of the brook, is a tall hawthorn, whose branches hang down like those of the weeping willow.

When we had sufficiently gratified our curiosity, we left these peaceful mansions of silence and solitude, and proceeded a quarter of a mile farther to Tina-Hinche, whither we had dispatched our coachman to bespeak break-fast. After a dish of tea and eggs, the customary fare of Ireland, we ordered the horses to be put to, and continued our *route* to the water fall in Lord Powerscourt's park.

What we had hitherto seen was very, pleasing and delightful: every half mile we advanced a new scene was presented to us.———But from Tina-Hinche to the water-fall we were enchanted with our journey. The hawthorn hedges on each side the road, were in full bloom and perfumed the air with their sweetness. The prospect was agreeably diversified with well-cultivated fields, beautisul groves, and rising mountains, ornamented with numerous enclosures.

When we approached the water-fall we vere struck with amazement. The astonishing accounts we had heard of this phœnomenon, conveyed no adequate idea of it to our minds. It descends from a steep rock of the stupendous height of 350 feet. In its fall, its appearance resembles the drifting of snow, and the spectators are bedewed with the spray at a considerable distance. After a copious shower of rain, the whole rock is covered; which must exhibit a more astonishing, the not a more beautiful appearance, than that we were eye-witnesses of. We did not satisfy ourselves with viewing it from below, but ascended by a winding path under frightful impending precipices, from which there is a continual dropping, and enjoyed a prospect of it from every passible paint of view. To behold it from the top of the rock, from, whence it takes the desperate leap, will seize the strongesd head with dizziness.

The ascent from hence to the top of mountain *Juice*,[24] whence it derives its source, is gradual, but continued for four miles.

We proceeded a mile up the hill, and had a god view, tho' not a very distinct one, of the Sugar Loaf Hill, Dublin Bay, and all the plain country.

We were fully bent upon gratifying out curiosity, and resolved to advance still higher, but the day being rather unfavorable for prospects, and one of our party becoming somewhat querulous, having a more important sense than that of light to gratify, we put a stop to our progress, and descended the hill much more rapidly than we had ascended it.

We had given orders for a dinner at Tina-Hinch, and by the exercise we had undergone in climbing the hill, our stomachs had acquired a wonderful keenness. However, when we arrived at the Inn, our host had made very litile prepa-

24   Djouce Mountain. —Ed.

ration for our entertainment. After waiting as patiently as circumstances would permit for the space of an hour, the table was covered with a wet cloth, blunt knives, and the following dishes of meat served up, viz. A piece of salt beef garnished with long greens, and which seemed to have been suspended ten years in the smoak; three chickens, and a quarter of lamb, without any kind of sauce or vegetables.

The waiter was a most original Hibernian character, and beggars description. His expressions and allusions were peculiar to himself. When we expostulated with him upon the badness of our dinner, his reply was, "upon my shoul it is very well you get any at all;—it is no fault of mine; for I am only a lodger." When we desired him to bring us a few more eggs, he said "we might as well ask a Highlander for a pair of Breeches as ask him for eggs." We begg'd he would go to a neighbour's house and buy a few—his reply was, "upon my shoul I could not buy one if I gave a ton of coals for it."

As we had nothing to induce us to a long continuance here, we made for Dublin with all pollible expedition, varying our road however, and leaving Bray a little to the right, passing thro' Lochlin's s town and Black Rock, and arrived at our lodgings at half past nine o'clock.

We found our strength and spirits nearly exhausted by this excursion—our stock of patience and knowledge greatly increased.

As human happiness depends much more upon trifling accidents than great events, it becomes every one who is studious of his own tranquility, to render himself as callous as possible to the petty chagrins and disappointments of life.

To partake of such a homely repast, for instance, as our Tina-Hinch host gave us, with contentment and good humour, would be a means of furnishing our minds with these virtues against a a more important occasion. Human life itself is but an entertainment, and every well-bred person should accommodate himself to that portion which the master of the feast is pleased to assign him, without disquieting himself and others, by endeavouring to provide himself with more luxurious delicacies.

June the first. The occurences of this day may be related in few words.

Being a little fatigued with our Wicklow expedition, we sauntered away the whole morning at our lodgings. Our obliging friend and countryman Mr. P— came and gave us so hearty an invitation to dine with him, that there was scarcely a possibility of declining it.

We spent the afternoon at his house in recounting the wonders we had seen the preceding day, and in other amusements, and then retired, according to our usual custom, for the remainder of the evening, to enjoy ourselves at our own lodgings.

It is no inconsiderable blessing to have the mind open to the enjoyment of domestic comforts.——I know few whose feelings are so susceptible in this point as those of my good friend Mr. W——. Momentary diversions and relaxations we may meet with abroad; but durable and permanent felicity is to be found only at home. How I pity the man who is a stranger to this!

On the second we were conducted by our Hibernian Mentor, Mr. B——; to the Temple, a noble structure, but quite in its infancy, designed for the same purpose as that at London.

About four o'clock the Lord Lieutenant went to the house of Peers in wonderful state. In eternal parade and shew, his Lordship made a princely appearance.

We dined with our active little guide, who led us through several secret alleys to Stephen's Green. In our road thither, we had a melancholy opportunity of observing various horrid scenes of drunkenness, a vice which strongly characterizes the Irish. Perhaps this may be attributed to the intoxicating nature and cheapness of whisky, which is the favourite liquor of the vulgar in Ireland.

On the third, which was a charming morning, we were employed in viewing very delightful scenes. We went out of the city by the great north road. The suburbs of Dublin are certainly deserving of the keen satire of Mr. Twiss. The buildings are low, beggarly cabins, thatch'd with straw,

and very frequently have no chimnies. They are inhabited by creatures clad in rags and covered with filth; shoals of whom sat basking in the sun, without any other employment than the elegant amusement of clearing each other of vermin; all the different methods of performing which Mr. Twiss seems to have observed with peculiar pleasure, as well as accuracy, in the course of his travels thro' and Ireland.

When we had quitted the city, a fine rich country, beautifully interspersed with white villas, presented itself. About a mile from town we left the N. road, turning to the E. by Sir Edward Newnham's. This seat is very pleasantly situated near the road side, with a rich lawn before it, and a plantation, resounding with the melody of birds, behind.

We proceeded a mile further, and were astonished to find ourselves in full view of the bay. Close to the sea-shore is the Charter-school, for the reception of Popish children, and giving them a Protestant education. Government has granted for the present year thirty thousand pounds towards its support. They are admitted from six to ten years of age, and apprenticed to Protestant masters at sixteen.

Half a mile from hence is Marino, Lord Charlemont's habitation.[25]

---

25   Marino House, built in 1755, would be bought by the Christian Brothers in 1881, and in 1915 sold (along with surounding grounds) to the Dublin Corporation, which would de-

No description, however flattering, can equal the beauties of this place. It is situate on a rising ground, and to the S. and S. E. is a fine view of Dublin Bay, the hill of Howth, &c. and to the W. and S. W. Bray-head, the Sugar loaf hill and other high mountains. The house is small, but elegant, and contains many fine paintings, particularly one which represents Judas's repentance.

The ground is laid out in a most exquisite taste. The cassino, built at a small distance from the house, after the plan of the cassino at Naples, is the completest piece of architecture I ever beheld.

The form of it is round, supported by pillars of the Doric order, ornamented by the Composite style. At the top, on the S. side, are two admirable statues of Venus and Apollo; on the N. two of Ceres and Bacchus.

In the shrubbery is a fine Gothic temple, with windows of painted glass, and a floor of most beautiful marble. From the temple is seen the bay thro' a narrow vista. Before it is a piece of water, on which was a Carolina duck, a most delicate fowl about the size of a seal, adorned with a tuft upon its head, and exceeding bright scarlet about the eye.

In our return thro' the shrubbery, we pursued the dubious windings of a serpentine walk, and were charmed with the delightful harmony of the grove. The sweet throstle and the black-bird vied

---

molish it around 1920 to make way for social housing. —Ed.

in artless strains. We lamented that we had not more time to spend in these silent, philosophic shades.

Upon this occasion I could not help indulging my fancy in the following poetical effusion upon the season of spring, which presents these delicious scenes to our view.

> The ruffian cold of surly-winter ends,
> Etherial mildness on our plains descends;
> No genial Zyphyrs gladden nature's face,
> And fertilizing show'rs her bosom grace.
> Each fragrant herb, tree, fruit and namel'd flow'r,
> With swelling buds salute the vernal hour:
> How sweet to hear the music of the grove,
> Resounding with enraptur'd strains of love!
> To walk at eve, and list'ning catch the song
> That warbled flows from Philomela's tongue;
> Or, roaming, watch the ruminating sheep
> Recline in hurdled cotes to balmy sleep.
> When mounts Aurora in her gilded car,
> Sweet goddess! usher'd by the lucid star,
> When dewy myriads the green fields adorn,
> And grateful odours hail the roseate morn;
> How bless'd to see fair Flora spread her sweets,
> And blithly frisk amidst her lov'd retreats.
> T' imbibe the fragrance of her essenc'd breath,
> From flow'ry arbors, or the blooming heath:
> Such scenes as these Saturnian days renew,
> And sweet Elysium's meads arise to view!
> At this soft season may I spend my days
> In calm reflection and poetic ease,
> May gracious Heav'n to me the task assign
> To tend sweet flow'rs, or nurse the spreading vine,
> T'explore the beauties of the verdant spring,
> And grateful praises to its Author sing.

After this pleasing excursion, we returned to the noise and tumult of the city, and dined at C——s tavern, where the civility of the landlord compensated for the indifference of the accommodations.

In the evening we resorted to the Theatre, where was performed the tragedy of Cato. Our expectation being a little raised before, we were never less entertain'd with a dramatic performance. Rider, who acted the part of Marcus, was a decent character.

This excellent tragedy, which is replete with the most sublime and admirable sentiments, is more adapted for the retirement of the study, than to be heard upon the public stage. No actors can do it sufficient justice.

On the fourth went to divine service at the asylum for Magdalens, where these poor unfortunate creatures have an excellent opportunity of recovering from those fatal deviations from virtue, which have been the cause of their misery.

It is a small edifice, built at the united expence of Lady Arabella Denny and Dean Bailey, an Anglesey gentleman. These two excellent persons, who go hand in hand in all charitable works, were the chief promoters of that truly humane institution the Foundling Hospital.

We dined at Mr. P——s, and attended evening service at St. Patrick's; returned to Mr. P——s to tea; and, after walking an hour at Stephen's Green, we retired toour own apartments.

On the fifth an expedition was planned by that honest veteran B—— senior, to visit the bleaching croft of Mess. G—— and Ph——. We took coach at eight o'clock, and arrived at Harlem to breakfast. It is situate about four miles W. of Dublin, near the hills, of which there is a prospect peculiarly beautiful from hence. After breakfast, we took a survey of the bleaching mills, in the construction of which much art and ingenuity is displayed. Returned to Dublin, and dined with Mr. Ph——.

A Captain of the Dublin volunteers entered. after dinner, and engaged us in warm conversation. Among other heterodox opinions of his, he would not allow that they took up arms merely to protect their country from invasion, and to preserve the internal peace of it, but for the redress of grievances: what these grievance are, no sensible, impartial person among them can tell: a military rage, or puerile fondness for the insignia of Mars, has broke out among their young men, and they endeavour to persuade themselves and others that they have real grievances to redress, whereas they exilt only in their own wild imaginations. If they make a prudent use of their arms, they will certainly be a blessing to their country; but should they be puffed up with self-important notions, and turn them against their mother country, they will inevitably prove its ruin. The natural situation of this kingdom is such, that it can never flourish but under the friendly protection of the British navy.

The only grievances that want redressing, arise chiefly from their own pride and laziness. If they could be prevailed on to shake off these, and strenuously cultivate the advantages they derive from nature, they could not fail to be a flourishing and happy people. Providence has distributed his blessings to them with a bounteous hand; their country, like Canaan, is a land of brooks of water, and its bowels contain inexhaustible treasures.

On the sixth we set out for Rath-Farnham, a seat of Lord Ely's, situate two miles S. E. of Dublin. This nobleman is a great admirer of the English taste. Here we saw a waggon, for the first time since our arrival in Ireland. Instead orf these, they use small cars, the diameter of whose wheel is scarcely two feet; their load about twice as large as that of an English wheel-barrow. Nothing shews more strongly the ridiculous lengths to which the *amor patriæ* is carried by the Irish, than their persevering, contrary to every principle of interest and common sense, to use these absurd vehicles, which were invented by their fore-fathers, in the infancy of the mechanical arts.

Their noddies are equally ridiculous and Inconvenient. These are a kind of one horse chaise, from which there is no prospect but that of a greasy driver's back, who plants himself upon a box of nearly the same elevation as the seat of the carriage, close to the person he drives.

*Risum teneatis amici?* A person unacquainted with the Irish character, would suppose that they either had no intercourse with the neighbouring countries, or that they were a people of such consummate honesty as to make a conscience of stealing from them even the least improvement.

In the lawn before Lord Ely's house, are three figures placed on a pedestal, by which is represented the rape of the Sabines. Not far from these is the stable, where Oliver Cromwell held its first parliament in Ireland. To the S. is a small grove, with a circular edifice supported upon eight columns, which serves as an aviary. It is stocked with a great variety of peacocks, silver and golden pheasants, a swan, muscovy ducks, &c. The latter of which very much resemble, in gait, a fat alderman.

On the N. side are his gardens, which are very extensive, and have several fruitwalls moderately furnished wish trees. His collection of plants and pinery are no objects of an Englishman's curiosity. The green-house is by far the most magnificent one I ever beheld. The dimensions of it are about one hundred and twenty feet long by thirty, and it is built brick.

The appearance of the house without is simple; within it is elegant and costly; it is furnished with a few antique busts, and several excellent paintings both ancient and modern. Some of the most remarkable are the following, viz. A representation of Mary Magdalen washing our blessed Saviour's feet, and wiping them with the hair of her head; the Ascension, the Apotheosis of Hercules, the Grecian Daughter supporting her imprisoned father's life with the milk of her breasts; a fruit and fowling piece, &c.

From the bow-window in the long room is a fine view of the bay, and other delightful objects. At the W. end of it is a very pleasant prospect of rising hills, clad with verdure, and interpersed with white buildings, which add life and beauty to every scene in the environs of Dublin.

In the afternoon we returned to the city, and dined at Mr. P———s, where a Dublin Volunteer had the politeness to present Mr. T——— with a ticket for the masquerade. The remainder of this evening, and the ensuing morning till seven o'clock; was such a scene of hurry; noise and confusion, as we had hitherto been total strangers to.

The unintermitting rattling of carriages, the hoarse shouts of the populace, commanding them to stop for inspection, the thick clouds of dust which filled every apartment in the more public parts of the city, rendered it an unfit habitation for any thing but that lawless tribe with which the streets were lined.

Here I cannot help observing that, the immediate tendency of masquerades is to banish all virtue, modestly and decency out of the world.

Ye Hibernian fair, hitherto renowned for conjugal fidelity, be cautious how open these dangerous inlets of matrimonial discord and wretchedness. Let not the baleful influence of example induce you to sacrifice the lasting joys of domestic happiness, for the transitory madness of an evening.

On the seventh we went to the courts of justice, where the ce'ebrated Mr. Burgh was haranguing upon a point of law with great eloquence and professional knowledge: he has much of the gentleman in his style and manner. Mr. Yelverton is blunt and vehement.

We dined at Mr. G———s. This gentleman has travelled much in England, to which he is as partial as a real native, who has confined himself within the limits of his own island, is to Ireland. He is amazed, like the clown in Virgil, at his former prejudices and stupidity.

Urbem *quam* dicunt Roman, mælibee, putavi, *stultus ego buic notræ similem.* It is the misfortune of those who have never stepped beyond the boundaries of their on parish, to be as strongly attached to the errors and absurdities as the excellencies of their country: and one good effect of travelling is, that it wears off these narrow prejudices, and gives the mind a more enlarged and generous way of thinking.

A person, who, by frequenting the London taverns, has acquired a delicate taste in eating, finds himfelf uncomfortably situated in Dublin. The Londoners are extremely neat, and can accomodate every taste to its satisfaction. Here excess of delicacy is a troublesome companion. A little philosophy is very requisite, and he that consults his own tranquility, must resolve before hand to take persons and things as he finds them. With this resolution we on the eight visited Mr. C—s tavern a second time, and dined as contentedly as pampered epicures would have done upon all the luxuries of the London, Grecian or Devil taverns.

We passed the afternoon very agreeably with our placid, good-natured friends, Mr. and Mrs. P———, From hence we walked ro Ranelagh, and saw a very curious exhibition of fire-works. The temple was peculiarly beautiful.

The music in different parts of the garden had a most delightful effect, particularly that which came from a tree, half a dozen musicians being placed among its branches.

On the ninth Mr, W——— and myself attended the debates of the house of the Commons, where we were truly mortified by that most insiped and tedious of all haranguers Sir L——— O———n, of whom it may be literally affirmed that he *spoke* a great deal, and *said* nothing. He sawed the air with his hand in a most unmerciful manner. Whoever has seen this honorable gentleman, will readily allow that graceful action is of no small importance even to a senator. There is no accomplishment, so easily acquired, of equal use and ornament. The, possessor of it neither disgusts his hearers, nor exposes himself to their ridicule. It adorns the gentleman, and adds weight and energy to the words of the orator.

We dined with our honest friend Mr. B——
senior. His wife is the neatest old person I ever
beheld. She conversed upon various subjects in a
very rational manner. Her loyalty to his Majesty
is almost unexampled. In delivering her sentiments concerning him, she expressed herself as
follows: "Poor King! I pity him; for he is a good
man, and deserving of better subjects than the
generality of Englishmen are. I envy his virtues,
but not his situation, nor would I change with
him if the crown was offered me this moment."

We were determined to be as acquainted with
Dublin as possible. For this reason we often
changed our tavern; and on the eleventh we were
recommended to the Eagle in Eustace-street,
frequented by the duke of Leinster, as something
very capital. But too sanguine expectations generally meet with disappointment. A couple of
chickens and a dish of pease were brought us,
which furnished abundant exercise for our patience and our teeth. The chickens might have
been hatched seven winters ago, and the pease
gathered as many days.

Aster taking a dish of tea at Mr. P——s, we
went to the house of Commons, under the protection of Sir John Blacquire. We heard nothing worthy our notice, except the delightful repetitions of
counsellor Tydd, and the incomparably facetious
motion of Sir H——y H—tst——e, which made the
house resound with a peal of laughter, a talent
which that baronet is peculiarly happy in.

The tongue is a most fruitful source of both pleasure and pain. How truly venerable is that person, who has acquired the noble art of wielding this small weapon with such dexterity as to make it at the same time instruct and delight the listening audience.

My worthy friend W——— and I went to a popish mass-house. The superstition of the poor wretches, who frequently kissed the floor; the inexpreslibly ridiculous fopperies of the priest, and the indecent filthiness of the place, gave us such an abhorrence of popery, as excited in us a mixture of indignation, pity and contempt. O popery, what hast thou to answer for, in thus fettering and enslaving the human mind!

In quitting the mass-house, we were followed by a person of some consequence in the congregation, who was very much chagrined at our not kneeling with the rest of the people. He accosted us in the following language. "Gentlemen, the next time you visit this place, I hope you will conform, in the exterior part at least, to our form of worship". We, thinking the dirtiness of the place a sufficient apology, took very little notice of his reproof, and wished him a good morning. How happy did we find ourselves in exchanging this mansion of ignorance and superstition: for the established church, which, though it pretends not to perfection, is undoubtedly a most decent, rational and edifying form of divine worship.

We dined, according to our usual custom on the sabbath, at Mr. P——s. Attended evening service at the Roundchurch, (*nomen ex vero ductum*) paid a farewell visit to the delicious walk of Stephen's Green, and, after spending an hour at Mr.P——s, returned to our lodgings.

On the twelfth we passed the morning in preparing for England; dined and drank tea at Mr. G——s, and retired early to our apartments, where we enjoyed a comfortable repose till four o'clock.

Now we are about to take our leave of Dublin, it will not be improper to add a word or two concerning this large and flourishing metropolis, as well as a few observations upon the country and inhabirants of Ireland, the city of Dublin, &c.

The city of Dublin is a strange mixture of grandeur and meanness. Many of its females exhibit a true representation of the city itself, who appear finely decorated about the head, with their feet and legs quite bare. It is upwards of three miles long, and nearly as many broad, and contains about 200,000 inhabitants. The river Liffey divides it into two equal parts, over which are built five bridges, of these Essex and Queen's only are worth mentioning.

The city is surrounded with a better circular road, about eight miles round. The principal streets are flagged, but, for to the most part ill- paved.

The police of Dublin, though certainly improved in many particulars, is still capable of very great additions. To perfect this, they are continually employed in making usesul regulations.

If we look a few years back, no further than 1775, we find their poor without any provision, except the casual charity of individuals. The streets were crowded with beggars, and every where you were presented with scenes of distress painful to behold.

To remedy which, they have instituted a house of Industry, where any one, who is found soliciting relief in the streets, is liable to be sent.

Another resource for protestant poor are the weekly collections made in all the parish churches, of which there are eighteen in Dublin, and two cathedrals. But these are by no means an adequate provision for them, at least far inferior to that humane and compleat one which is made for the poor in England. Their paupers, consider the house of Industry as a place of confinement, rather than as an asylum from the wretchedness of poverty, and it is with extreme reluctance they sacrifice their native liberty, slothfulness and dirt, to the comforts which it affords.

As to the country of Ireland, it seems to have but two of what we may properly call natural defects; viz. a scarcity of coal and timber: though, perhaps, even these might be remedied by industry. The want of timber is to be attributed solely to the inattention of former ages, who were continually engaged in wars and civil broils, in neglecting the plantation of oak trees. That the soil of Ireland will produce them, is evident from several edifices built chiefly of Irish oak, in which this island abounded in former ages; and certainly no cause can be assigned why the same may not still be raised.

This country is excellently watered, and their waters abound with the best of fish: no island in Europe, probably in the known world, can boast of a finer river than the Shannon.

Ĩ here is also in Ireland great plenty of very commodious harbours, which is a singular advantage to trade and commerce.

Most of the useful arts of life, though they have of late years made a rapid progress, are here still in their infancy, when compared to that astonishing degree of perfection they are at in the neighbouring kingdoms.

The principal manufactures they excel in are those of linen, tabinets, and stuffs. The woollen manufacture is what they are very little acquainted with, nor is it ever likely to become an advantageous concern to them, notwithstanding their present laudable efforts to vie with the English in this article.

The White-boys, so called from wearing their shirts over air clothes, and the Oak-boys, denominated from wearing a branch of oak in their hats, have long been a baneful pest to lreland.

The objects of their vengeance are chiefty gentleman who raise their estates, terants who take such eslates, and tithe gatherers. They assemble in numerous bodies, and commit the most horrid outrages upon their persons and property. The volunteers, whose design is to preserve the internal peace of the kingdom, as well as to guard it against foreign invasion, have great merit in quelling these lawless tribes, and will, no doubt, in time, entirely extirpate them. The Irish volunteers amount in as whole to about 50,000.

If these gentlemen apply their military talents to the noble purposes they have hitherto been engaged in, they will shortly enjoy the happiness of becoming powerful instruments in promoting the welfare and prosperity of their country. If, on the contrary, they prostitute them in the cause of rebellion, and madly abuse this privilege, as their ancestors did, in the reign of Elizabeth, it is odds but they will again relapse into the barbarity and wretchedness they were for centuries immersed in.

As to the tempers of the Irish in general, they are an open, generous, lively, intrepid people, and much inclined to hospitality. This is the bright side of their charater. The most predominant vices among them are drinking, swearing, and rioting. The lower classes among them have not the least regard to cleanliness; this half virtue, as Aristotle stiles it, they can scarcely be thought to have any idea of; a little attention in this particular would render them far less disgusting to others, and more comfortable to themselves.

Their ladies are furnished with every polite accomplishment, but seem more studious of finery than neatness. They walk extremely well, but are not very remarkable for beauty. The French manners seem to be the original they copy after. Painting is become fashionable among them—seperations and divorces are scarcely ever heard of.

A spirit of extravagance, or living above their income, pervades every class of people among them. It has insensibly descended into the lower ranks, who wear two coats at a season when they have no occasion for one, and always cover a copious head of hair with a wig.

The climate of Ireland, though perfectly healthful, is a wet one; being surrounded with large bodies of water, and abounding in lakes. It rains more or less five days in the week, as is proved by actual observation.

The protestant cause daily gains ground, by reason of the Foundling-hospital, the Charter-school, and many other admirable institutions of the same kind. The superiority of papists, however, throughout the kingdom is as three to one, or perhaps somewhat more; in the city of Dublin, it is in the proportion of five to one.

On the thirteenth we walked down to George's-quay, and embarked, at half past six, A. M. on board the *Hillsborough*, Captain Parry; weighed anchor about half past seven, and sailed, with a gentle westerly breeze, taking a farewell retrospect of the city, and enjoying a delightful view of the hill of Howth and Lambey Island, on the one hand,—Black Rock, Dunleary, Bray-head and the Wicklow mountains on the other.

About fix P. M. a brisk gale sprung up, and wafted us, in perfect safety, to our deflined harbour, Holy-head, at a little past eight.

Here we were under the necessity of taking up our residence for this night, on account of the dilatoriness of the King's officers in examining our trunks.

We regaled our squeamish stomachs with excellent mutton broth, a quarter of lamb, and lobsters, which fish the Holyhead coasts abounds in, of the largest sort.

On the fourteenth, at eight in the morning, we took coach for Gwindu, where we arrived at half past ten, and breakfasted in a most comfortable manner. Travellers are here accommodated with so much ease, neatness, and civility that they generally continue, as long as their circumstances will permit them.

The melody of the harp, which no well frequented Inn in this country is without, receives additional charms from the pleasing behaviour of the good-natured hostess. But as we had other objects in view besides studying our own tranquility, we had sufficient resolution to quit it, and engaged a chaise to convey us from hence to that most stupendous curiosity Paris mountain.

When we travelled this island; I could not help imagining at every step I advanced, that I trod upon inchanted ground. It will not admit of a doubt but this is the Mona of the ancients, as is very clearly proved by the ingenious author of *Mona antiqua restaurara.*[26] The surface of it is not remarkable for fertility, abounding with rocks, and being extremely bare of timber; but within its bowels are contained immense treasures. The copper-mines at Paris mountain are exceedingly valuable, as well as curious. The works bear some resemblance to a large cathedral supported by massy pillars, having, numberless cloysters and recesses.

After abundantly gratifying our curiosity in this wonderful place, we directed our course to Porthamlwch, a harbour completely formed by nature, in a rock; where the tide rises to a considerable height, and is accessible to loops, which convey from hence the riches of the mountain. The ore is prepared and brought hither at the small expence of four shillings and sixpence per ton.

We dined at a small village of the same name, in a beautiful lodge belonging to the reverend Mr. H——, who has a very considerable property in the mines of Paris mountain, and returned at night to Gwindu.

On the fifteenth we took leave of our obliging hostess at nine o'clock; and proceeded to Porth-llongdu, in the eastern part of the island, which is supposed to have derived its name from the circumstance of the Romans landing there

26   Henry Rowlands (1655 - 1723). —Ed.

with a black ship: *llong* signifying, in the ancient British language, *ship*, and *du*, black. This is the residence of the reverend Mr. H——, who shewed us in his pasture the traces of a temple of the venerable Druids. After dining at his house, in company with the pleasing Mrs. Sp—row, &c.; we set out for Porth-aithwy, making Price's in our road, from whence we had a delightful view of the Caernarvonshire hills, which were beautifully gilded by the sun from the western hemisphere. Even Snowden, that king of mountains, condescendet to lay aside his dusky cap, and display his venerable head, a favour with which few travellers are distinguisned.

Conway was the next place of our destination, where we arrived at ten o'clock, and-complered thiedey's journey.

On the sixteenth, as our accomodations a here were but very indifferent, we were glad to leave it as foon as possible, and accordingly crossed the ferry at seven o'clock. We returned from hence exactly by the same route we came, and our progress was so very rapid, owing to our impatience for home, that we made few observations during the remainder of our Journey, except this—— that our own country can lose nothing by being compared with the most fruitful and pleasant regions on the face of che globe.

One melancholy reflection, however, we could not help making that it is a great pity so fine a country should be inhabired by a people so insensible to their own happiness. *"O fortunati nimium sua si bona norint."*[27] Englishmen, not confcious of their happiness, instead of enjoying, with contentment and gratitude, the many pecuhar advantages which the bounty of Providence hath bestowed upon them, are ever employed in defeating, his gracious purposes, by their differentiations, factions and tumults.

In a mild climate, under a form of government still more mild; in a fertile country, productive of every thing delightful to the eye and pleasant to the taste; adorned with magnificent cities, beautiful towns and pleasant villages; how comfortable and happy might the lives of Britons be! Peace, unanimity and contentment at home, is all we want; these ever have, and, with the blesgig ot Providence, ever will procure us success and glory abroad, as wel as establish permanent felicity among ourselves.

Permit me, then, my countrymen and sellow-citizens, to conclude this small work with that pathetic exhortation of Virgil:

*Ne, pueri, ne tanta animis assuescite bella;*
*Neu patriæ validas in viscera vertite vires.*

Of which I beg leave to offer the following translation:

---

27 From Virgil's *The Georgics*: 'The farmers would count themselves lucky, if only they knew how good they had it'. —Ed.

Let not fierce wars, nor horrid discord's blaze,
Lay waste your country, and your cities rase;
Cease, cease, ye Britons, o'er yourselves to lord,
Noughte'er can Britain conquer, but the Brit-
ish sword.

## FINIS

# Index

www.ingramcontent.com/pod-product-compliance
Lightning Source LLC
Chambersburg PA
CBHW020347100426
42812CB00035B/3386/J

* 9 7 8 1 9 1 0 8 9 3 2 5 8 *